Brain Stretchers
Book 4

written by
Carolyn Anderson

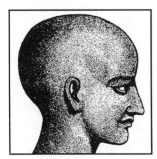

© 1998
CRITICAL THINKING BOOKS & SOFTWARE
www.criticalthinking.com
P.O. Box 448 • Pacific Grove • CA 93950-0448
Phone 800-458-4849 • FAX 408-393-3277
ISBN 0-89455-674-6
Printed in the United States of America

SQUARE MAGIC

Place the numbers 0, 1, 2, 3, 4, 5, 6, and 7 in the eight small circles so the sum of each side of the square will be 11.

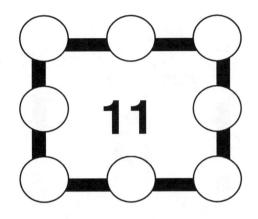

Place the numbers 0, 1, 2, 3, 4, 5, 6, and 7 in the eight small circles so the sum of each side of the square will be 12.

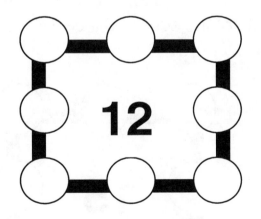

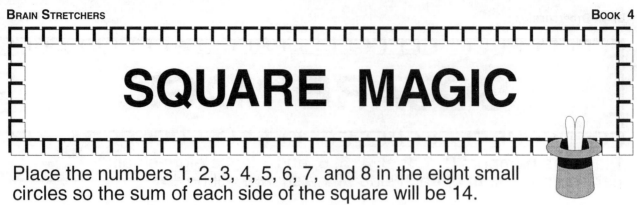

SQUARE MAGIC

Place the numbers 1, 2, 3, 4, 5, 6, 7, and 8 in the eight small circles so the sum of each side of the square will be 14.

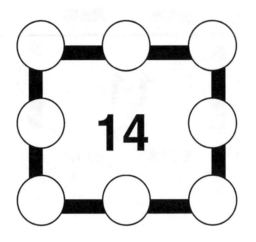

Place the numbers 1, 2, 3, 4, 5, 6, 7, and 8 in the eight small circles so the sum of each side of the square will be 15.

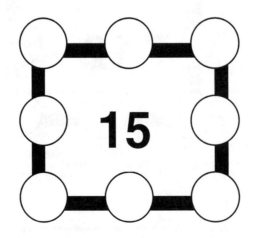

POLYGON MAGIC

Place the numbers 1, 2, 3, 4, 5, and 6 in the six small circles so the sum of each side of the triangle will be 12.

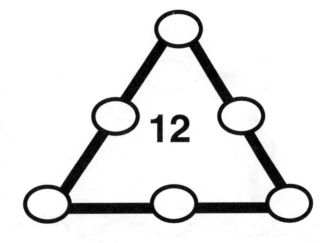

Place the numbers 1, 2, 3, 4, 5, 6, 7, and 8 in the eight small circles so the sum of each side of the square will be 13.

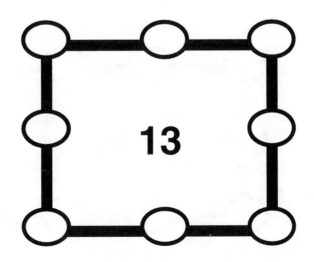

POLYGON MAGIC

Place the numbers 0, 1, 2, 3, 4, 5, 6, 7, 8, and 9 in the ten small circles so the sum of each side of the rectangle will be 16.

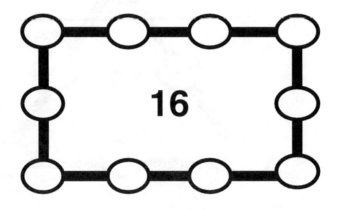

Place the numbers 1, 2, 3, 4, 5, 6, 7, 8, 9, and 10 in the ten small circles so the sum of each side of the rectangle will be 19.

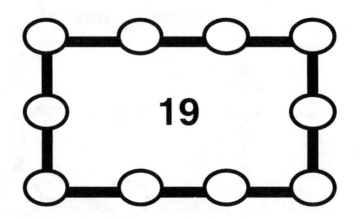

POLYGON MAGIC

Place the numbers 0, 1, 2, 3, 4, 5, 6, 7, 8, and 9 in the ten small circles so the sum of each side of the pentagon will equal 11.

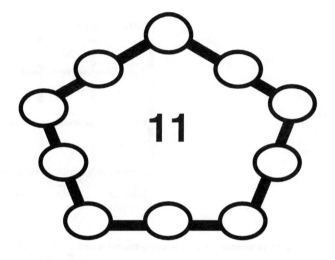

Place the numbers 0, 1, 2, 3, 4, 5, 6, 7, 8, 9, 10, and 11 in the twelve small circles so the sum of each side of the hexagon will equal 14.

SUM PROBLEM I

Place two different numbers in each row and column. Select from the numbers 1, 2, and 3. The total for each row and column is given. The correct solution has no more than two numbers in each row, column, or diagonal.

For example:

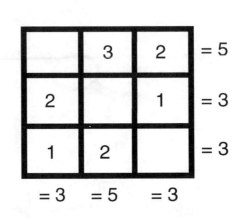

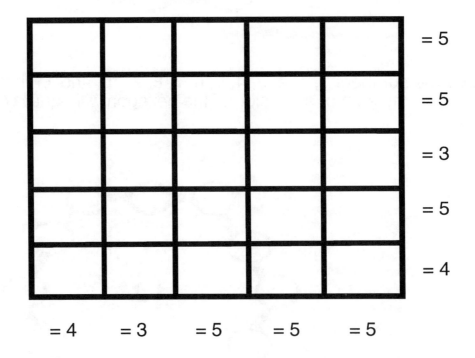

SUM PROBLEM II

Place two different numbers in each row and column. Select from the numbers 1, 2, and 3. The total for each row and column is given. The correct solution has no more than two numbers in each row, column, or diagonal.

For example:

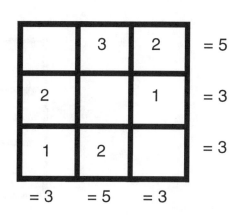

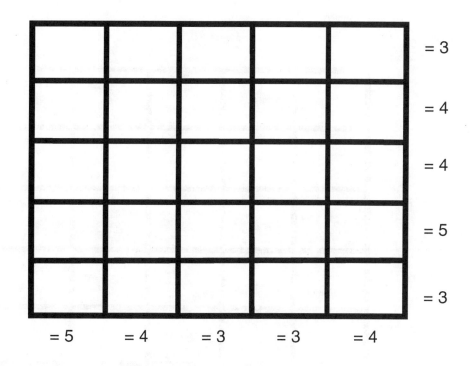

SUM PROBLEM III

Place two different numbers in each row and column. Select from the numbers 1, 2, and 3. The total for each row and column is given. The correct solution has no more than two numbers in each row, column, or diagonal.

For example:

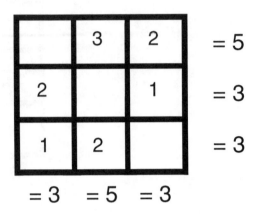

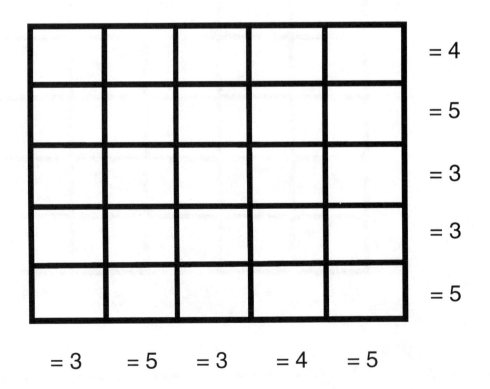

PERFECT 100!

If all 10 questions are answered correctly, the total will be 100!

3, 7, 10, 11, 12, 17, ___   _____

Number of rings in the Olympic Symbol   _____

Number of factors of 48   _____

Number of prime numbers from 1 to 100   _____

What is 1/2 of 1/4 of 1/5 of 120?   _____

Sum of all the numbers on a clock face divided by 13   _____

Number of 9s in the answer to 12,345,679 times 81   _____

What is a gross divided by a dozen?   _____

What is the number of degrees in a right angle minus the number of piano keys?   _____

Degrees Fahrenheit at which water freezes divided by the number of quarts in a gallon   _____

TOTAL = 100

AN EQUATION THING

Place any number from 0 to 9 in the empty squares to make true equations in the rows and columns. Equations are worked left to right or up to down, and no negative numbers are allowed.

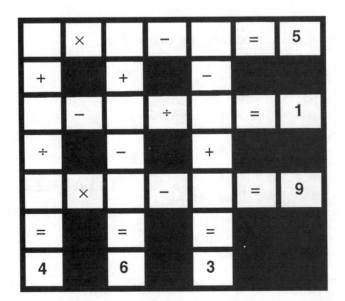

AN EQUATION THING

Place any number from 0 to 9 in the empty squares to make true equations in the rows and columns. Equations are worked left to right or up to down, and no negative numbers are allowed.

	×		÷		=	5
+		÷		+		
	×		−		=	2
÷		×		−		
	+		−		=	2
=		=		=		
4		9		7		

	−		×		=	8
÷		−		+		
	×		÷		=	1
+		+		−		
	+		−		=	2
=		=		=		
6		9		5		

AN EQUATION THING

Place any number from 0 to 9 in the empty squares to make true equations in the rows and columns. Equations are worked left to right or up to down, and no negative numbers are allowed.

Grid 1:

	×		÷		=	4
+		+		×		
	+		−		=	5
÷		÷		−		
	+		+		=	9
=		=		=		
2		8		9		

Grid 2:

	+		÷		=	5
×		×		+		
	+		×		=	8
÷		×		−		
	+		−		=	4
=		=		=		
6		8		1		

MAKE AN EQUATION

Place 2, 3, 4, 12, or 24 in the squares below and +, −, ×, or ÷ in the circles to make true equations. No number is to be used more than once in any equation (e.g., 12 × 2 + 3 + 4 = 31).

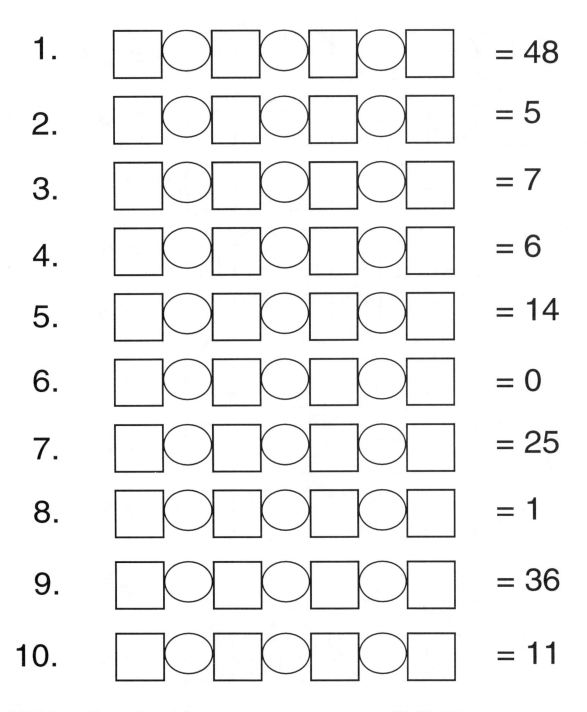

1. ☐○☐○☐○☐ = 48

2. ☐○☐○☐○☐ = 5

3. ☐○☐○☐○☐ = 7

4. ☐○☐○☐○☐ = 6

5. ☐○☐○☐○☐ = 14

6. ☐○☐○☐○☐ = 0

7. ☐○☐○☐○☐ = 25

8. ☐○☐○☐○☐ = 1

9. ☐○☐○☐○☐ = 36

10. ☐○☐○☐○☐ = 11

MAKE AN EQUATION

Place 2, 3, 4, 6, or 24 in the squares below and +, −, ×, or ÷ in the circles to make true equations. No number is to be used more than once in any equation (e.g., 6 × 2 + 3 + 4 = 19).

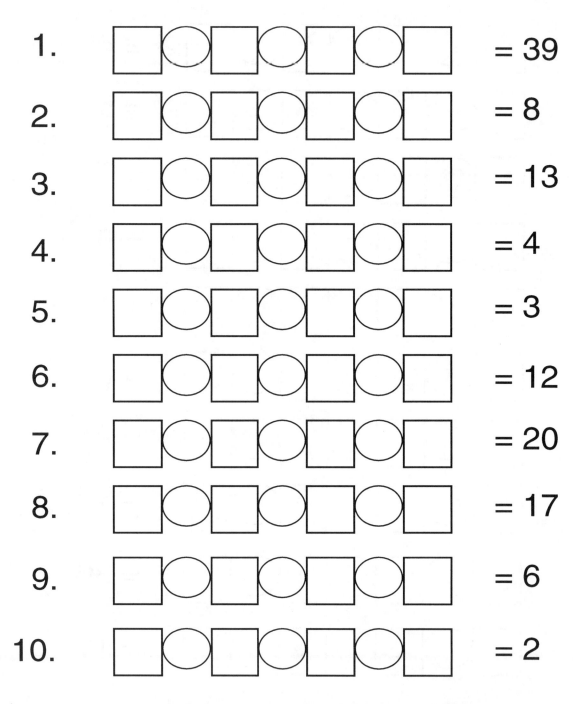

1. ☐○☐○☐○☐○☐ = 39

2. ☐○☐○☐○☐○☐ = 8

3. ☐○☐○☐○☐○☐ = 13

4. ☐○☐○☐○☐○☐ = 4

5. ☐○☐○☐○☐○☐ = 3

6. ☐○☐○☐○☐○☐ = 12

7. ☐○☐○☐○☐○☐ = 20

8. ☐○☐○☐○☐○☐ = 17

9. ☐○☐○☐○☐○☐ = 6

10. ☐○☐○☐○☐○☐ = 2

MAKE AN EQUATION

Place 2, 3, 6, 8, or 24 in the squares below and +, −, ×, or ÷ in the circles to make true equations. No number is to be used more than once in any equation (e.g., 24 ÷ 8 + 6 + 3 = 12).

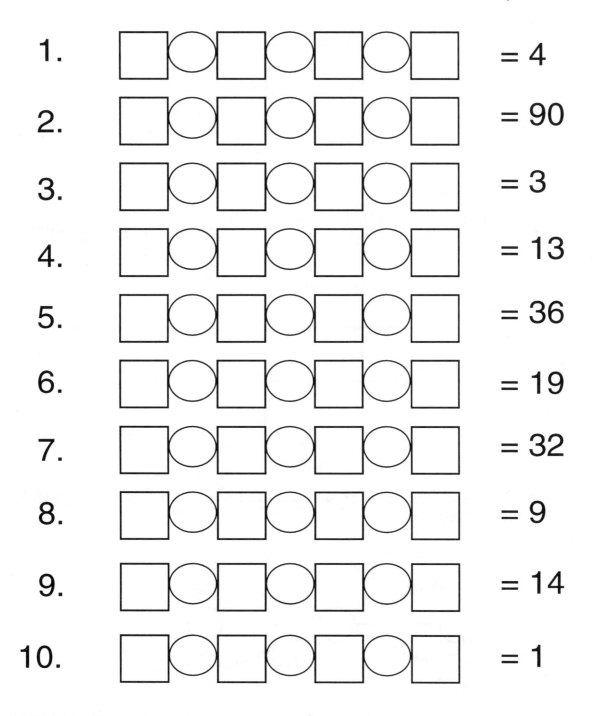

1. ⬜ ◯ ⬜ ◯ ⬜ ◯ ⬜   = 4

2. ⬜ ◯ ⬜ ◯ ⬜ ◯ ⬜   = 90

3. ⬜ ◯ ⬜ ◯ ⬜ ◯ ⬜   = 3

4. ⬜ ◯ ⬜ ◯ ⬜ ◯ ⬜   = 13

5. ⬜ ◯ ⬜ ◯ ⬜ ◯ ⬜   = 36

6. ⬜ ◯ ⬜ ◯ ⬜ ◯ ⬜   = 19

7. ⬜ ◯ ⬜ ◯ ⬜ ◯ ⬜   = 32

8. ⬜ ◯ ⬜ ◯ ⬜ ◯ ⬜   = 9

9. ⬜ ◯ ⬜ ◯ ⬜ ◯ ⬜   = 14

10. ⬜ ◯ ⬜ ◯ ⬜ ◯ ⬜   = 1

AN EQUALITY THING

Place the numbers 0, 1, 2, 3, 4, 5, 6, 7, and 8 in the nine squares below. If placed correctly, the sum of each row, column, and diagonal will be 12.

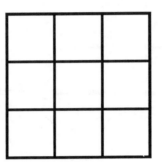

Place the numbers 1, 3, 5, 7, 9, 11, 13, 15, and 17 in the nine squares below. If placed correctly, the sum of each row, column, and diagonal will be 27.

Place the numbers 0, 1, 2, 3, 4, 5, and 6 in the seven circles so each of the three lines has the same total.

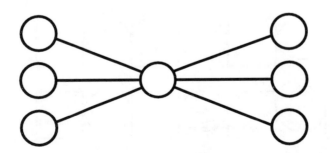

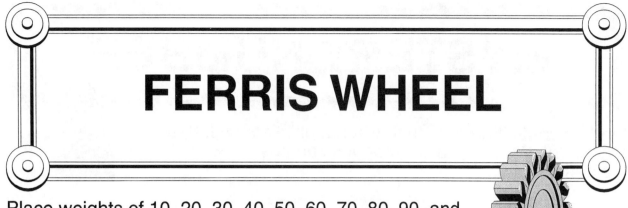

FERRIS WHEEL

Place weights of 10, 20, 30, 40, 50, 60, 70, 80, 90, and 100 pounds in the ten small squares so the sum of any two weights next to each other equals the sum of the two weights directly across.

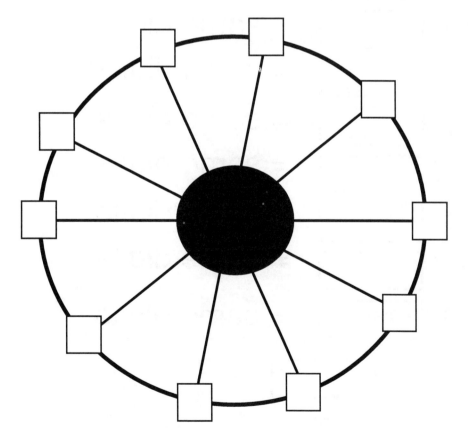

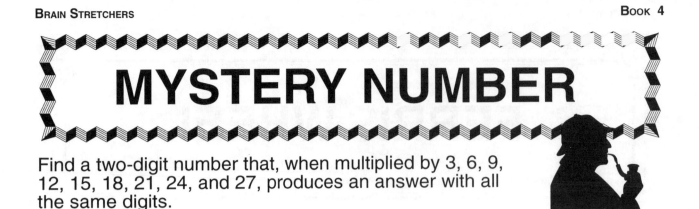

MYSTERY NUMBER

Find a two-digit number that, when multiplied by 3, 6, 9, 12, 15, 18, 21, 24, and 27, produces an answer with all the same digits.

3 X [   ] = same digits

6 X [   ] = same digits

9 X [   ] = same digits

12 X [   ] = same digits

15 X [   ] = same digits

18 X [   ] = same digits

21 X [   ] = same digits

24 X [   ] = same digits

27 X [   ] = same digits

[   ] = ?

MULTIPLICATION MATCH

Correctly place the given numbers to make a true multiplication problem. All the numbers given must be used, and no number may be used more than once.

X

1.

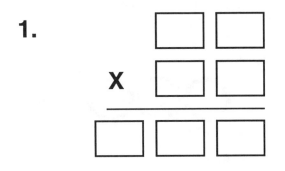

1, 2, 4, 5, 6, 7, 8

2.

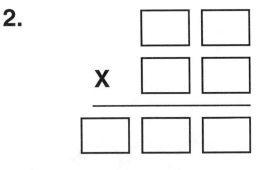

0, 1, 2, 5, 6, 7, 8

3.

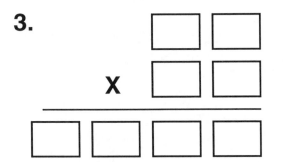

1, 2, 3, 4, 5, 6, 8, 9

MULTIPLICATION MAGIC

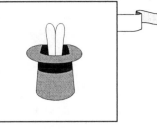

Place the numbers 1 – 9 (1, 2, 3, 4, 5, 6, 7, 8, and 9) in the nine small circles to make a true equation. No digit may be used more than once.

◯◯◯ x ◯◯ = ◯◯◯◯

Now, try another one ...

◯◯◯ x ◯◯ = ◯◯◯◯

BOOMERANG MATH

Put the new result in the blank provided. See if it matches the number you started with.

1. Select a mystery number _____
   Double it _____
   Subtract 2 _____
   Multiply by 4 _____
   Divide by 8 _____
   Add 1 _____

2. Select a mystery number _____
   Add 5 _____
   Add twice the mystery number _____
   Add 1 _____
   Divide by 3 _____
   Subtract 2 _____

3. Try to make a series of commands that will result in the originally selected number being the answer.

   _____   _____
   _____   _____
   _____   _____
   _____   _____
   _____   _____

ALWAYS 1

#1

Put the new result in the blank provided.

1. Select a mystery number   _____
    Subtract 3   _____
    Multiply by 3   _____
    Add 10   _____
    Subtract 3 times the mystery number   _____

2. Select a mystery number   _____
    Add 4   _____
    Add 3 times the mystery number   _____
    Divide by 4   _____
    Subtract the mystery number   _____

3. Try to make a series of commands that will result in an answer of 1.

    _____   _____
    _____   _____
    _____   _____
    _____   _____
    _____   _____

BORDER MAZE

	OK!	
1		2
4		3

Write a 1, 2, 3, or 4 in each area below from start to finish. Make sure the same numbers are not placed in areas that touch each other. They cannot even touch at corners. You may start from anywhere.

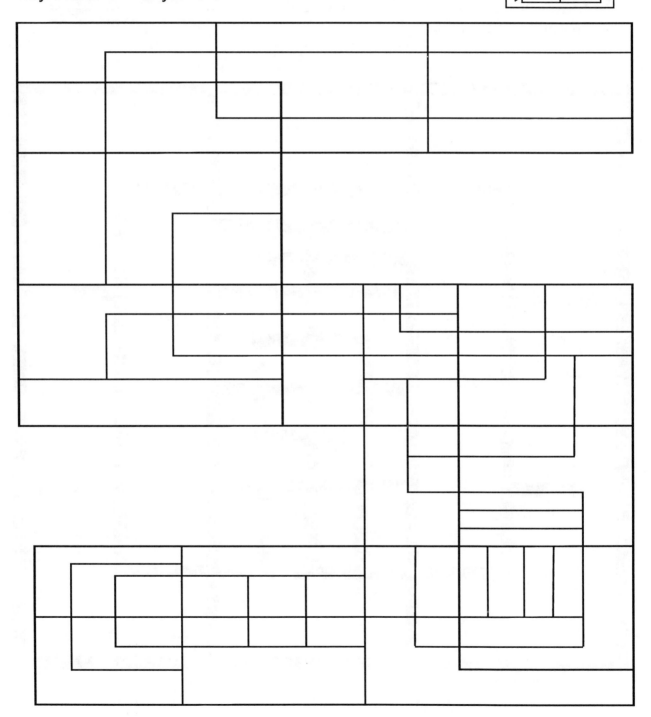

MAP MAKER

Use only 4 colors (or numbers 1–4) to shade in the different areas in the figure below. No area with the same color (or number) can border another with that same color (or number). Same colors (or numbers) can't touch even at a corner. When 4 corners meet, all 4 areas must be different.

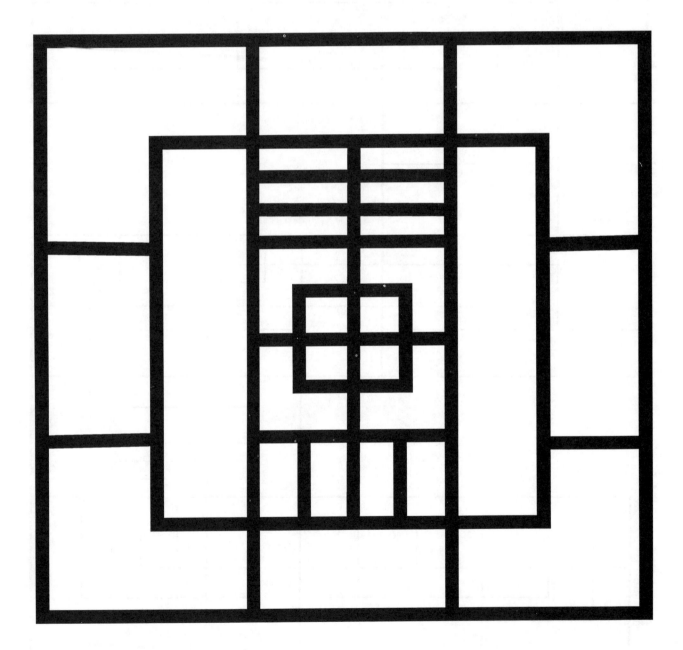

MAP MAKER

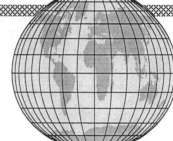

Use only 4 colors (or numbers 1– 4) to shade in the different areas in the figure below. No area with the same color (or number) can border another with that same color (or number). When 4 corners meet, all 4 areas must be different.

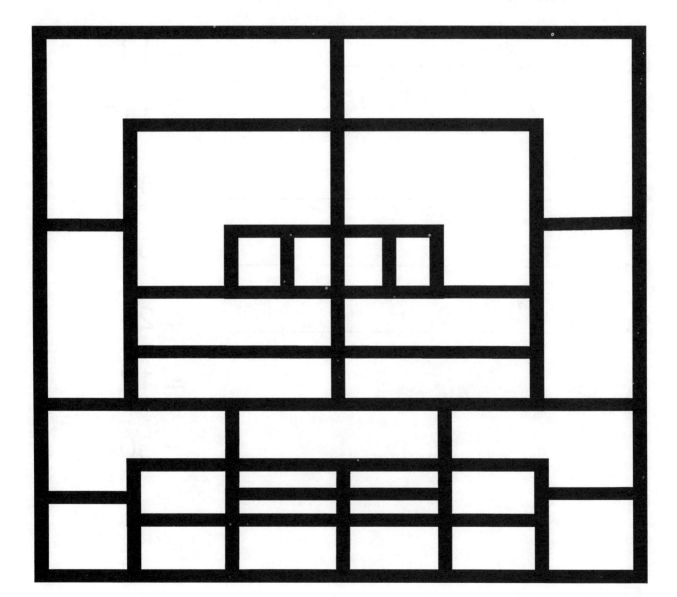

IT TAKES FIVE!

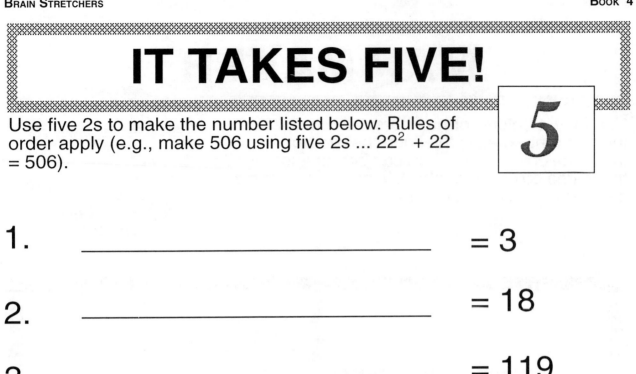

Use five 2s to make the number listed below. Rules of order apply (e.g., make 506 using five 2s ... $22^2 + 22 = 506$).

1. _____ = 3

2. _____ = 18

3. _____ = 119

4. _____ = 42

5. _____ = 34

6. _____ = 26

7. _____ = 12

8. _____ = 30

IT TAKES FIVE!

5

Use five 3s to make the number listed below. Rules of order apply (e.g., make 180 using five 3s ... $3(33 + 3^3)$).

1. _____ = 11

2. _____ = 1

3. _____ = 36

4. _____ = 363

5. _____ = 31

6. _____ = 44

7. _____ = 15

8. _____ = 51

IT TAKES FIVE!

5

Use five 4s to make the number listed below. Rules of order apply (e.g., make 84 using five 4s ... 44 + 44 − 4 = 84.

1. _____ = 22

2. _____ = 56

3. _____ = 21

4. _____ = 40

5. _____ = 107

6. _____ = 8

7. _____ = 14

8. _____ = 32

COMMON NUMBERS

EVERYDAY
THINGS

Listed below are 11 commonly known numbers with initials used instead of the words (e.g., 12 = "I. in a F." is really "12 Inches in a Foot." Figure out what the initials stand for.

1. 12 = M. in a Y.

2. 30 = D. in S., A., J., and N.

3. 180 = D. in a T.

4. 3 = M. of the S.

5. 5 = S. on a P.

6. 15 = D. in A. before T. is D.

7. 1 = N. of M. the E. has

8. 9 = I. in a B. G.

9. 5 = D. in a Z. C.

10. 9 = S. C. M.

11. 3 = F. in a Y.

COMMON NUMBERS II

EVERYDAY THINGS

Listed below are 11 commonly known numbers with initials used instead of the words (e.g., 12 = "I. in a F." is really "12 Inches in a Foot." Figure out what the initials stand for.

1. 52 = W. of the Y.

2. 50 = S. on an A. F.

3. 7 = O. of the W.

4. 5 = P. in a G. P.

5. 8 = M. F.

6. 3 = W. on a T.

7. 32 = P. on a C.

8. 3 = R. in a N.

9. 6 = S. on a D.

10. 2 = L. on a H.

11. 9 = S. S. D.

COMMON NUMBERS III

EVERYDAY THINGS

Listed below are 11 commonly known numbers with initials used instead of the words (e.g., 12="I. in a F." is really "12 Inches in a Foot." Figure out what the initials stand for.

1.   4 = W. D.

2.   25 = C. in a Q.

3.   24 = H. in a D.

4.   11 = S. on a S. B. A. D.

5.   13 = O. U. S. C.

6.   3 = K. who L. their M.

7.   9 = C. L.

8.   5 = R. in the O. S.

9.   3 = R. in a C.

10. 24 = K. in P. G.

11. 13 = B. D.

FIND A PATTERN

By figuring out how many squares are in a small figure, you can find a formula for discovering how many squares are in a large figure. You can put the formula into practice for large figures. Or you can simply count squares.

$x + 3 =$

$x + 3 =$

$x + 3 =$

$x + 3 =$

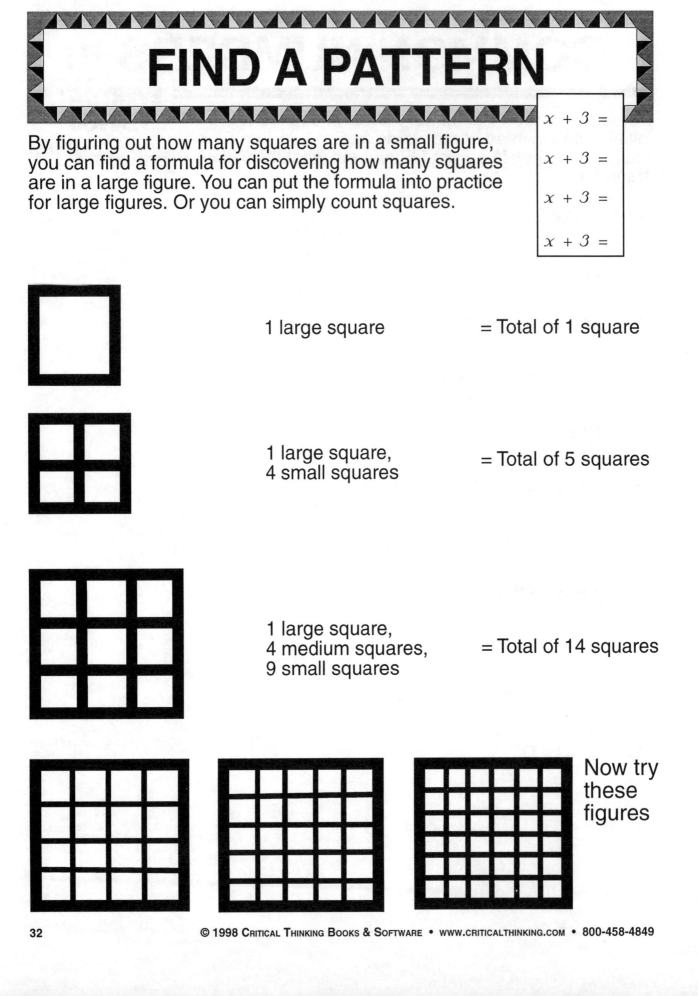

1 large square   = Total of 1 square

1 large square,
4 small squares   = Total of 5 squares

1 large square,
4 medium squares,   = Total of 14 squares
9 small squares

Now try these figures

BLASTOFF

Draw a line through each instance of 987654321 in the puzzle below. Locate this sequence in a line horizontally, vertically, and diagonally, listed forwards or backwards. The sequence appears many times.

```
9 1 2 3 4 9 8 1 2 3 4 5 6 7 8 9
8 9 2 8 7 6 6 3 4 1 2 3 4 9 8 7
1 2 3 3 5 3 9 1 2 8 9 1 2 3 9 8
2 1 2 3 4 5 8 3 9 8 2 2 3 4 8 7
3 1 2 5 6 5 4 8 8 1 2 3 4 5 7 6
1 2 3 1 1 5 6 7 7 3 2 4 1 9 6 1
3 4 3 2 6 2 6 7 5 4 3 5 6 8 5 2
4 5 6 7 8 9 3 5 8 6 1 6 7 7 4 3
5 4 8 1 2 3 4 4 5 9 2 7 8 6 3 4
6 9 4 5 1 2 3 4 5 6 7 8 9 5 2 5
7 9 3 4 3 9 8 7 6 6 8 9 1 4 1 9
8 8 2 2 3 5 1 2 3 4 7 3 2 6 7 8
9 7 1 2 7 4 3 2 1 1 1 8 5 8 9 7
5 6 1 8 6 7 8 5 9 8 2 4 9 5 7 9
7 8 9 6 9 8 7 6 5 4 3 2 1 4 3 8
1 2 3 4 5 9 4 5 6 2 4 1 1 2 3 7
2 2 7 6 7 8 9 2 1 6 5 6 1 2 4 6
1 2 3 4 5 4 3 2 3 5 6 8 7 8 9 5
9 8 7 4 1 2 3 4 5 6 7 8 9 1 2 4
1 2 3 4 5 4 6 7 8 9 8 7 6 5 3 6
5 5 4 3 5 6 1 2 3 4 9 8 7 6 5 5
6 6 1 6 9 8 7 6 5 4 3 2 1 1 6 4
7 7 7 2 4 5 7 8 8 9 3 2 1 2 7 3
8 8 2 1 3 4 6 5 9 8 7 6 5 4 8 2
9 9 4 9 8 7 6 5 8 3 1 2 3 4 9 1
```

MATH WORD MAZE

Find and draw a line through the following words in the maze below. If located correctly, the answer will resemble the meaning of the word.

1. division
2. minus
3. line
4. angle

5. compass
6. horizontal
7. vertical
8. diagonal

9. triangle
10. rectangles
11. parallelograms
12. circle

```
        A N I V I S I O N D I M I
      L L T D A N C O E N I L H O R
      V A E L A T N O Z I R O H T E
      D I N T R I A C C I T C E R R
      D L I O V I I   E M A I N S L
      A A N G G H R   L P N G L E O
      R C V E R A T C M D A I A G O
      M I N U S E I O T C I S P A R
      T T R I R C C D D I T U S I O
      A R C U M P A H O R I E A N G
      D E I Z U N E R I A N G L T R
      E V C I G L E P     A L L E L
      E V E C A O     R U E R O O
                    A A S T G N
                  P S M A R
                V E C A N G
                R E C V E R
                A N C O M H
                O R I C O M
                M I N H O R
                V E R T L I
                D I V D I A

                J I T R I A
                P A R O L O
```

NUMBER SOUP

Find twenty words for numbers (e.g., one) in the soup below, listed in a straight line forward, backward, or diagonally.

```
              O I S T W E O
          H G I F O R S E R H U N S
      S Y T R I H T O U D E R D N U H E I G
    E I S I M I L E F H R Z M E I C T H F O T H O
  T H O M I L N S I G G O N O F O U S Z T U S I
U M I L I E O N E H E W I O L O W T E R W M I L Z
E I S L L W T O V O E N I E N I O L I M E S I F E
X T E W L E O N E T R M R T W E L V E O N W L I W
O E N F I Z N E N X H Z O U R X O V O W T Z N D X
  O R Z O V W V I E T Y T R O F I O H U Y E R W
  E R O N E I E M I X E R O T F O S F I F T Y O
      M I L F A T H O U S A N D O N U N T
          O E O S O X E Y T N O W T
              I O R E X I N
```

MATH WORD CODE

Figure out what letter each picture represents. Match each letter to its corresponding picture to figure out the 7 math words below. Hint: Trophy = T

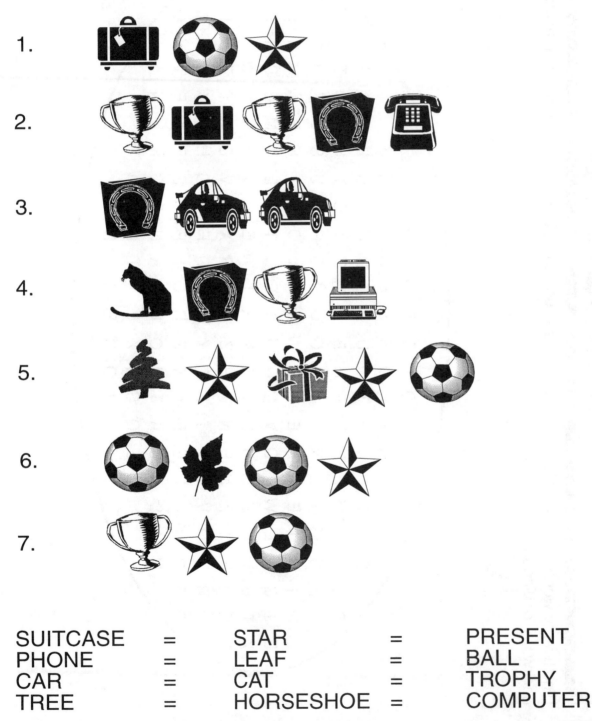

1.

2.

3.

4.

5.

6.

7.

SUITCASE	=	STAR	=	PRESENT	=
PHONE	=	LEAF	=	BALL	=
CAR	=	CAT	=	TROPHY	=
TREE	=	HORSESHOE	=	COMPUTER	=

MATH WORD CODE

CLASSIFIED

Figure out what letter each picture represents. Match each letter to its corresponding picture to figure out the 7 math words below. Hint: Suitcase = E

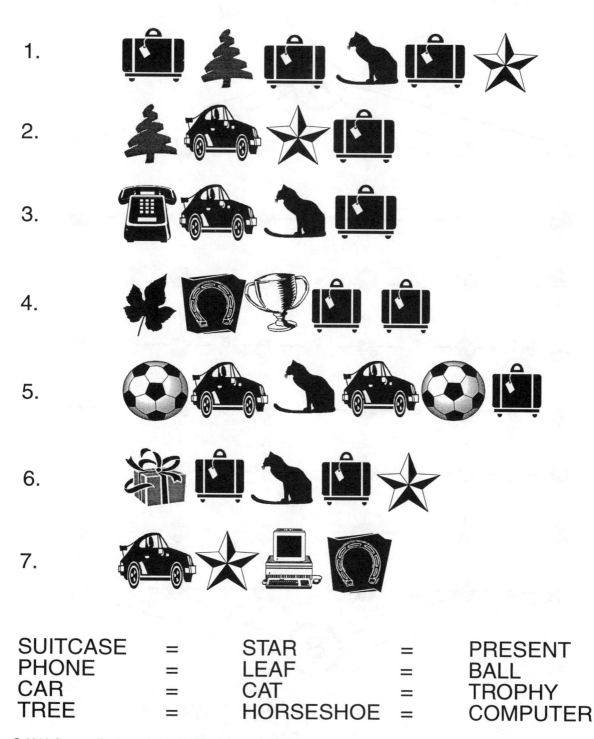

SUITCASE   =   STAR   =   PRESENT   =
PHONE   =   LEAF   =   BALL   =
CAR   =   CAT   =   TROPHY   =
TREE   =   HORSESHOE =   COMPUTER   =

ROAD MAP I

Select 3 highways out of a possible six (1, 2, 3, 4, 5, or 6). Move from City A to City B along only those 3 selected highways. Only one path is correct. (Example: If you decide to travel on highways 1, 2, and 3, then you can move only to those numbers.)

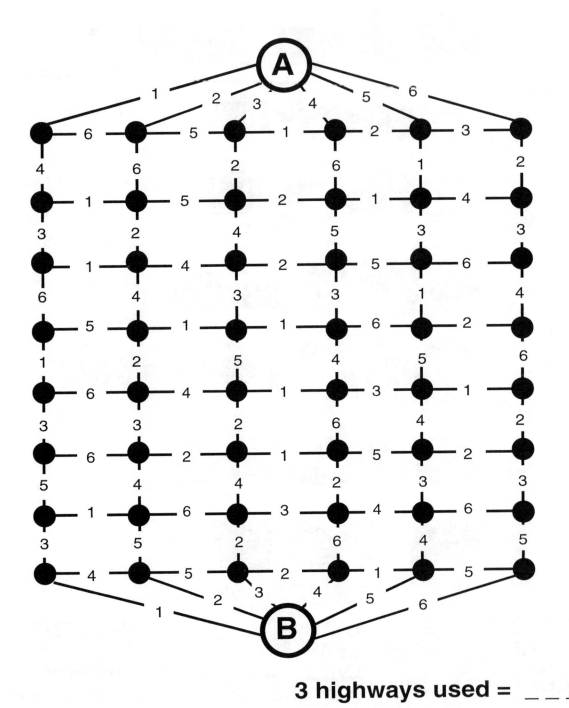

3 highways used = _ _ _

ROAD MAP II

Select 3 highways out of a possible six (1, 2, 3, 4, 5, or 6). Move from City A to City B along only those 3 selected highways. Only one path is correct. (Example: If you decide to travel on highways 1, 2, and 3, then you can move only to those numbers.)

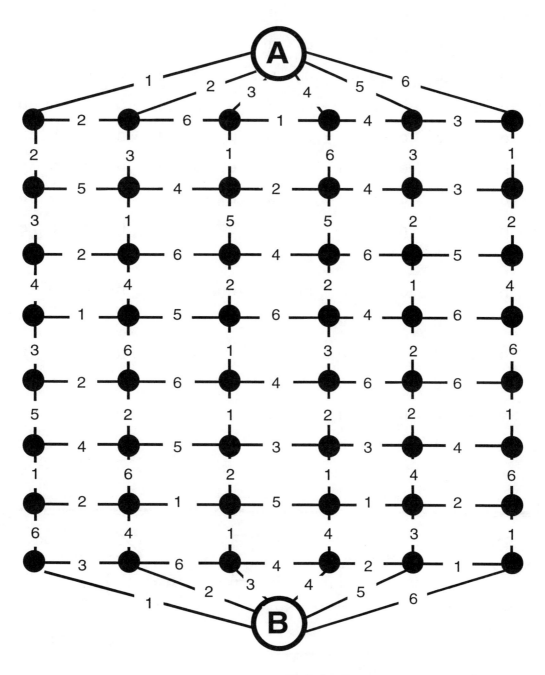

3 highways used = _ _ _

SEE AND CIRCLE

Find and circle 20 math terms that are indicated in the box below. Some items may represent more than one term (fraction, numerator, and denominator). Terms can be found in straight horizontal, vertical, or diagonal lines.

```
d  i  o  z  e  p  a  r  t  a  n  u  c  i  d  e  c  i
m  u  l  r  i  g  h  n  u  m  e  r  a  t  o  r  s  e
d  i  v  s  q  u  e  l  c  r  i  c  p  e  r  c  u  m
p  m  u  l  t  i  p  l  i  c  a  t  i  o  n  m  b  a
a  n  o  i  t  c  a  r  f  d  p  o  i  n  t  i  t  r
r  a  l  o  d  e  f  n  r  a  e  c  t  d  e  c  r  g
s  q  u  a  r  e  c  o  b  e  r  c  o  a  r  a  a  o
l  q  p  a  r  a  a  i  n  o  c  o  i  l  d  e  c  l
s  i  o  p  e  r  t  s  s  u  e  o  i  m  e  t  t  e
u  d  n  c  q  c  a  i  m  e  n  d  e  n  a  o  i  l
b  e  i  e  u  r  v  v  a  t  t  r  a  p  l  o  l
r  o  o  d  c  i  r  i  g  h  t  a  n  g  l  e  n  a
r  o  o  s  d  t  e  d  e  n  o  m  i  n  a  t  o  r
m  r  e  a  n  u  m  e  r  d  e  m  o  n  p  e  r  a
p  c  u  b  e  e  e  c  n  e  r  e  f  f  i  d  c  p
```

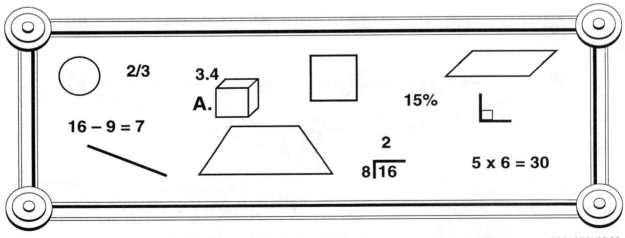

CARNIVAL TOSS

If a stuffed bunny is hit with a baseball and knocked off the shelf, you score the number of points listed on the bunny. Given 6 baseballs, circle the 6 bunnies that need to be knocked down to total 100 points.

CARNIVAL DARTS

At the carnival, a Grand Prize is awarded for popping 6 star balloons with 6 darts for a total of 100 points. Circle the 6 star balloons needed to total 100.

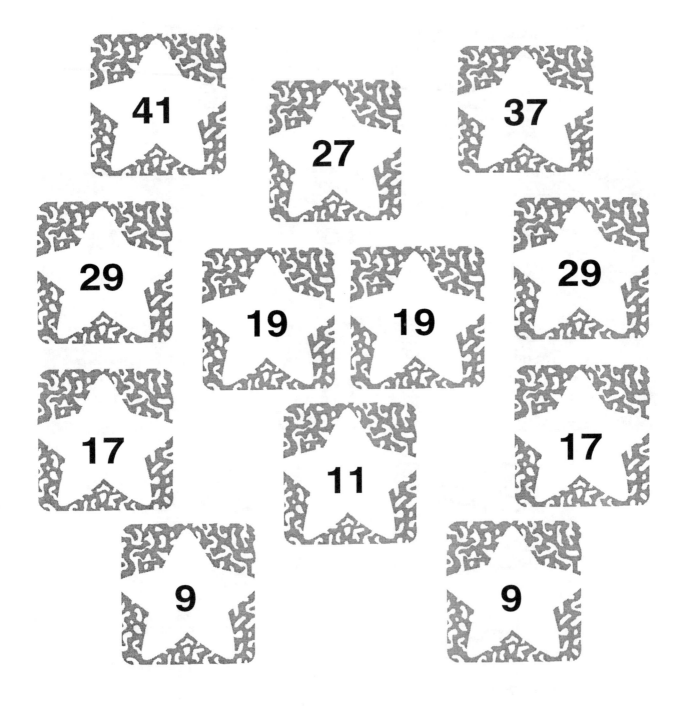

CARNIVAL DARTS

At the carnival, a Grand Prize is awarded for popping 6 balloons with 6 darts for a total of 100 points. Circle the 6 balloons you need to pop to total 100.

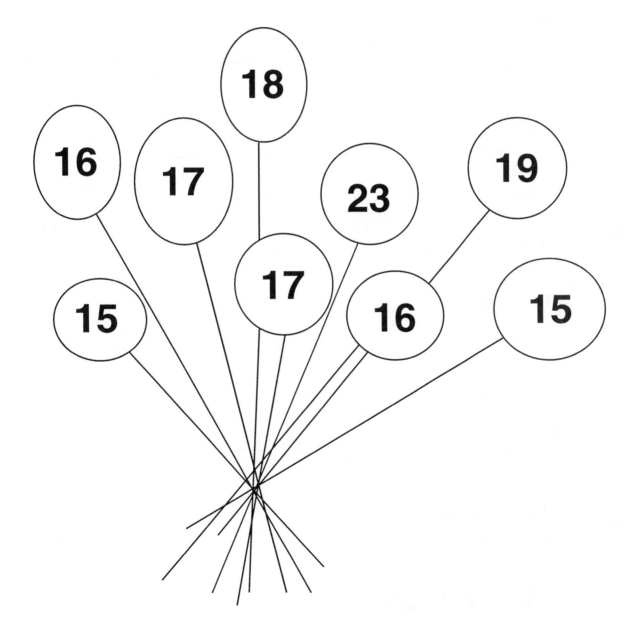

WHAT DOESN'T BELONG?

For each group, list the number that doesn't belong and what the others have in common. The sum of the numbers that don't belong is 50.

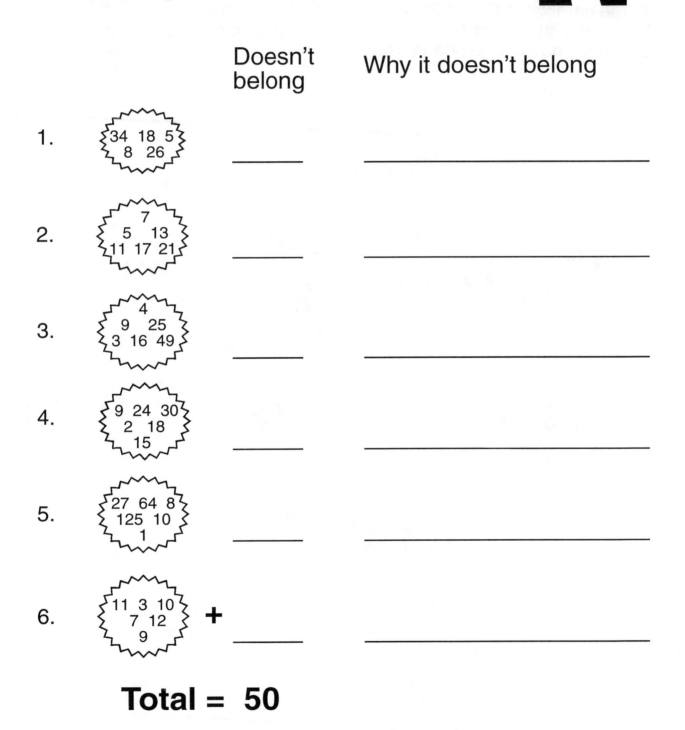

	Doesn't belong	Why it doesn't belong
1. 34 18 5 8 26	_____	_____
2. 7 5 13 11 17 21	_____	_____
3. 4 9 25 3 16 49	_____	_____
4. 9 24 30 2 18 15	_____	_____
5. 27 64 8 125 10 1	_____	_____
6. 11 3 10 7 12 9 +	_____	_____

Total = 50

CONNECTED TOTALS

Section the entire area into 4 separate connected parts with equal totals.

Example: Section the entire area into 3 separate connected parts with equal totals.

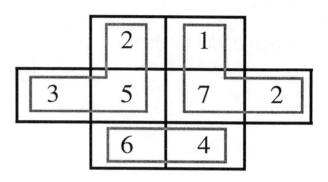

Now try it for real.

5	4	7	2	5	1
3	9	3	8	7	3
1	5	5	6	4	3
1	4	1	6	1	2

CONNECTED TOTALS

Section the entire area into 5 separate connected parts with equal totals.

Example: Section the entire area into 3 separate connected parts with equal totals.

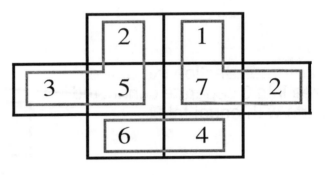

Now try it for real.

	2	4	1	
3	5	9	3	9
2	5	9	4	4
4	7	8	3	3
6	5	5	2	9
	3	3	7	

CONNECTED TOTALS

Section the entire area into 5 separate connected parts with equal totals.

Example: Section the entire area into 3 separate connected parts with equal totals.

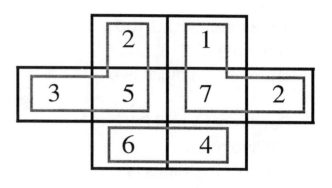

Now try it for real.

6	4			1	9
2	9	2	6	3	7
5	1	7	4	8	2
2	3	5	1	7	4
	2	1	6	3	

WHAT'S MY NUMBER?

On the blank provided, write the number indicated.

1.　　Between 20 and 100
　　　Multiple of 2, 3, and 5
　　　Sum of the digits is 6　　　　　　　　　　＿＿＿＿＿＿＿＿＿

2.　　Between 10 and 200
　　　Multiple of 7
　　　One of the digits is 0　　　　　　　　　　＿＿＿＿＿＿＿＿＿

3.　　Between 100 and 500
　　　When divided by 100, remainder is 20
　　　3 is not a factor
　　　8 is not a factor　　　　　　　　　　　　＿＿＿＿＿＿＿＿＿

4.　　Between 1 and 200
　　　Prime
　　　When divided by 9, remainder is 8
　　　One of the digits is 0　　　　　　　　　　＿＿＿＿＿＿＿＿＿

5.　　Between 50 and 150
　　　Multiple of 3
　　　Factor of 441
　　　Multiple of 7
　　　Sum of the digits is 12　　　　　　　　　＿＿＿＿＿＿＿＿＿

6.　　Between 75 and 200
　　　Multiple of 15
　　　Factor of 2700
　　　When divided by 10, remainder is 5　　　＿＿＿＿＿＿＿＿＿

WHAT'S MY NUMBER?

On the blank provided, write the number indicated.

1.   Between 50 and 100
       Multiple of 7
       Sum of the digits is 10   _____

2.   Between 20 and 200
       Multiple of 3
       Multiple of 5
       Odd number
       When divided by 11, remainder is 3   _____

3.   Between 1 and 150
       Multiple of 2, 3, 4 and 5
       Sum of the digits is 6   _____

4.   Between 100 and 300
       Multiple of 11
       Sum of the digits is 11   _____

5.   Between 200 and 300
       Prime
       Sum of the digits is 8
       When divided by 5, remainder is 1   _____

6.   Between 100 and 250
       Factor of 900
       Multiple of 15
       Sum of the digits is 9
       Odd number   _____

COLLECT 10

Move from the START to the FINISH, ending with a score of 10. If you pass through a square, add that number to your running total. If you pass through a circle, subtract that number from your running total. Negative numbers are not permitted, and numbers cannot be used more than once.

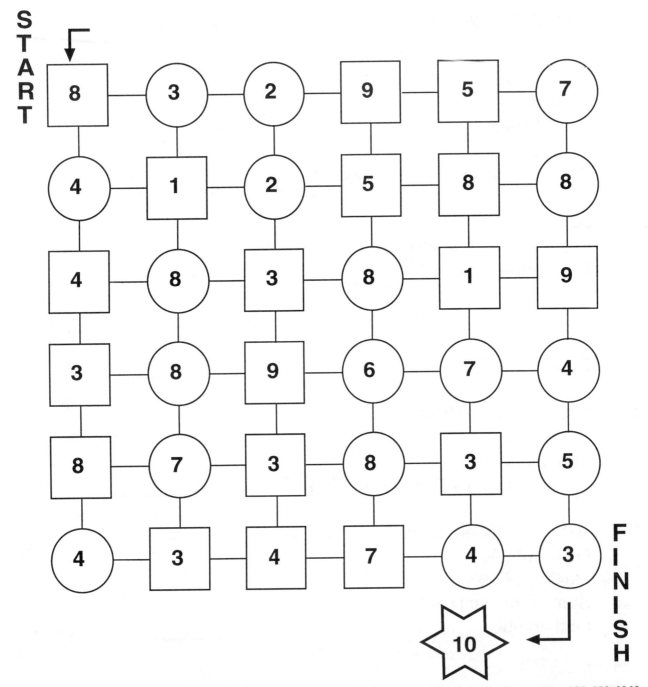

FIFTY IS NIFTY

Start at any corner and finish at any other corner. Add the number in each circle to your running total. Collect a total of 50. No circle may be entered more than once.

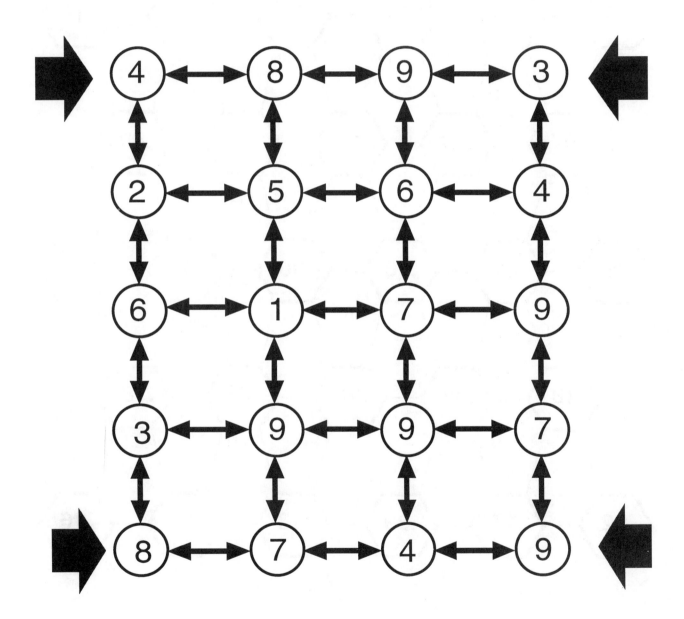

DOLLAR HUNT

Move from the top row to the bottom row collecting exactly $1. No number can be used more than once.

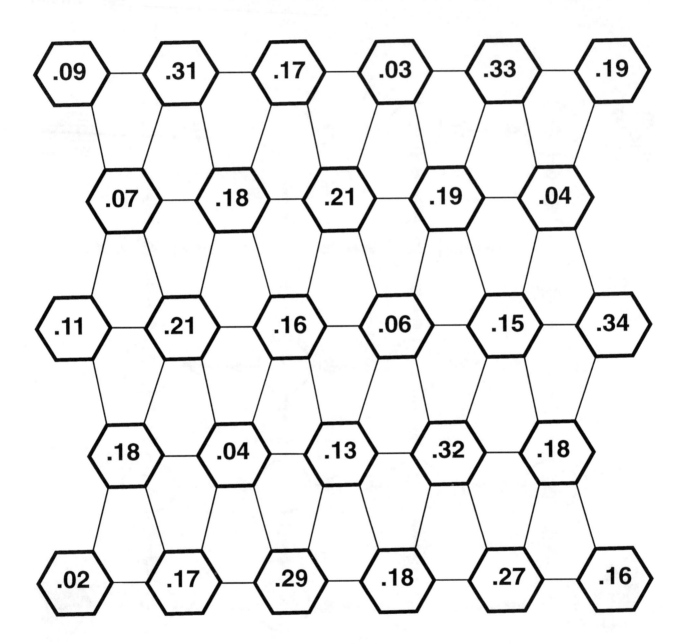

STATE OF CONFUSION

Use 3 separate lines to divide the box below into areas that contain the same number of houses.

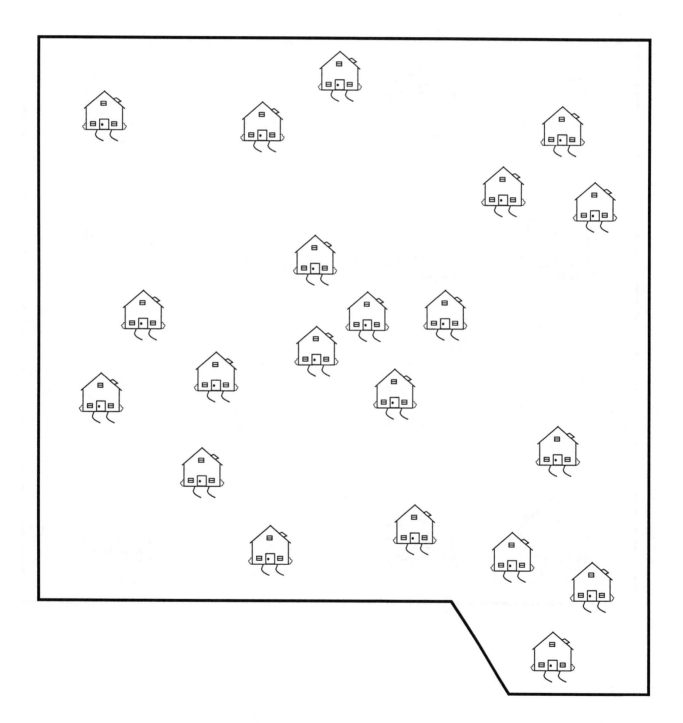

LAND DIVISION

Draw lines so that the box below is divided into 4 equal lots,
each the same size and shape and each containing 3 houses.

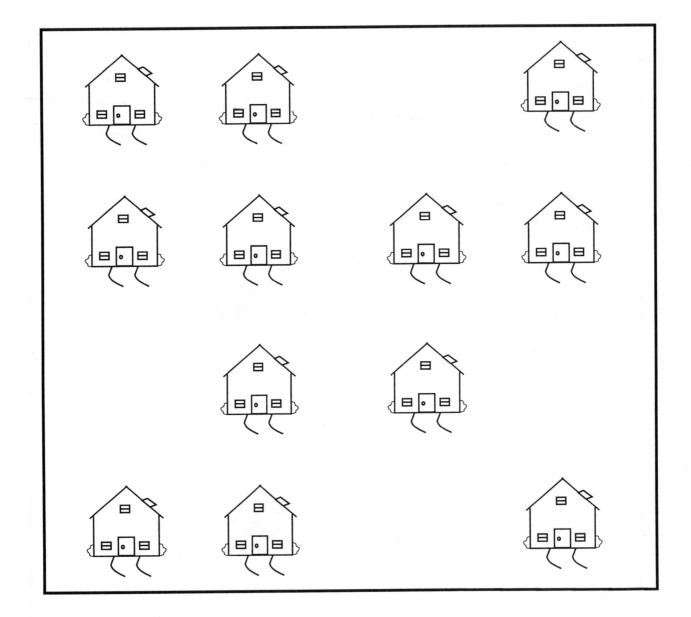

LAND DIVISION

Draw lines so that the box below is divided into 8 equal lots, each the same size and shape and each containing 1 house.

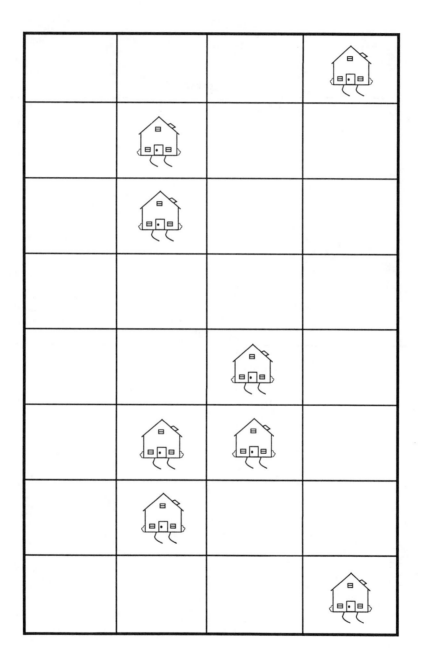

SQUARE DEAL

Find two sets of two-digit numbers such that if you reverse the numbers, their squares are reversed, too.

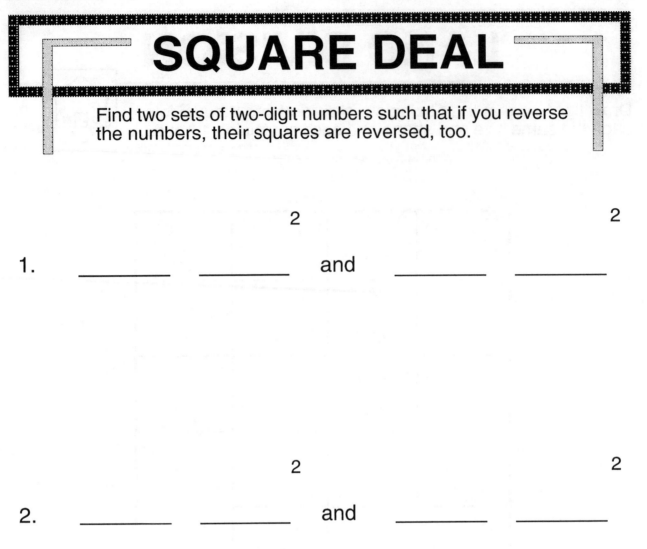

1. _____ _____ ^{2} and _____ _____ ^{2}

2. _____ _____ ^{2} and _____ _____ ^{2}

SQUARE IT!

Replace each blank with a digit from 1 to 9 to make a true equation.

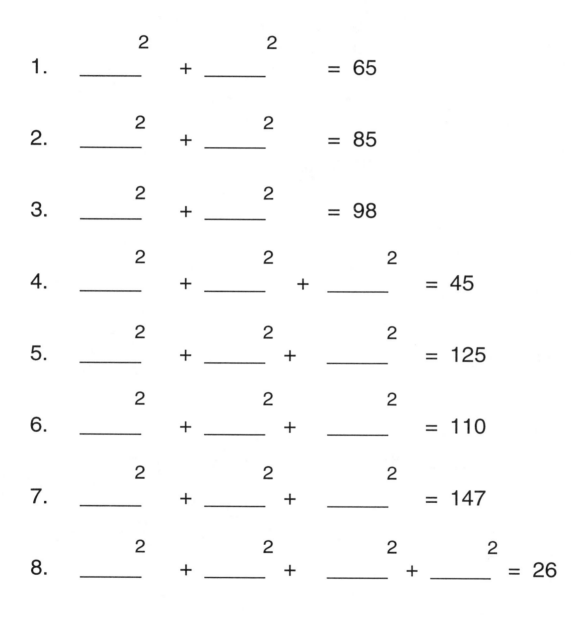

1. $\underline{}^2 + \underline{}^2 = 65$

2. $\underline{}^2 + \underline{}^2 = 85$

3. $\underline{}^2 + \underline{}^2 = 98$

4. $\underline{}^2 + \underline{}^2 + \underline{}^2 = 45$

5. $\underline{}^2 + \underline{}^2 + \underline{}^2 = 125$

6. $\underline{}^2 + \underline{}^2 + \underline{}^2 = 110$

7. $\underline{}^2 + \underline{}^2 + \underline{}^2 = 147$

8. $\underline{}^2 + \underline{}^2 + \underline{}^2 + \underline{}^2 = 26$

CUBE IT!

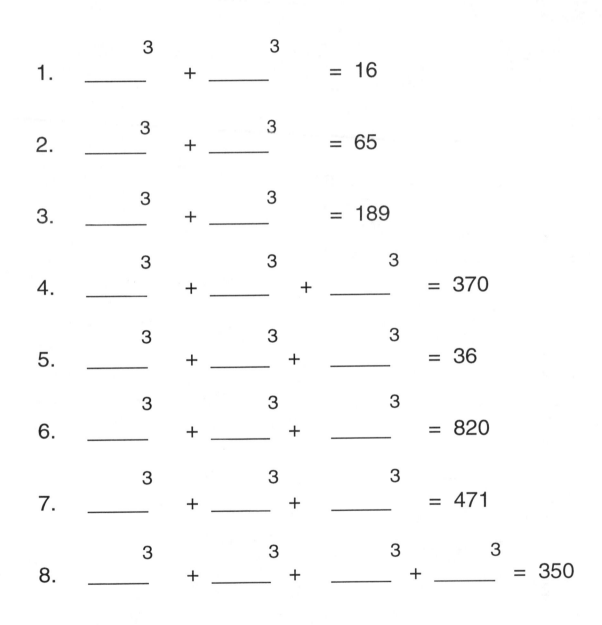

Replace each blank with a digit from 0 to 9 to make a true equation.

1. _____³ + _____³ = 16

2. _____³ + _____³ = 65

3. _____³ + _____³ = 189

4. _____³ + _____³ + _____³ = 370

5. _____³ + _____³ + _____³ = 36

6. _____³ + _____³ + _____³ = 820

7. _____³ + _____³ + _____³ = 471

8. _____³ + _____³ + _____³ + _____³ = 350

LUMBERJACK LOGIC
(a game for two)

During your turn, you may mark out as many trees as you want in any one of the 3 rows. The person who marks out the last tree is the loser. You must always mark out <u>at least one tree</u> during your turn.

LUMBERJACK LOGIC
(Try it again!)

During your turn, you may mark out as many trees as you want in any one of the 3 rows. The person who marks out the last tree is the loser. You must always mark out <u>at least one tree</u> during your turn.

ANSWERS

$a = \pi r^2$

$a^2 + b^2 = c^2$

$f = ma$

$e = mc^2$

PAGE 1

[11] (clockwise from top left):
4, 0, 7, 1, 3, 6, 2, 5

[12] (clockwise from top left):
7, 0, 5, 1, 6, 4, 2, 3

PAGE 2

[14] (clockwise from top left):
4, 2, 8, 1, 5, 6, 3, 7

[15] (clockwise from top left):
3, 4, 8, 1, 6, 2, 7, 5

PAGE 3

[12] (clockwise from top):
6, 1, 5, 3, 4, 2

[13] (clockwise from top):
1, 7, 5, 2, 6, 3, 4, 8

PAGE 4

[16] (clockwise from top left):
5, 2, 3, 6, 9, 1, 0, 8, 7, 4

[19] (clockwise from top left):
10, 2, 3, 4, 9, 6, 7, 5, 1, 8

PAGE 5

[11] (clockwise from top):
0, 8, 3, 7, 1, 6, 4, 5, 2, 9

[14] (clockwise from top): 0, 6, 8,
5, 1, 11, 2, 9, 3, 7, 4, 10

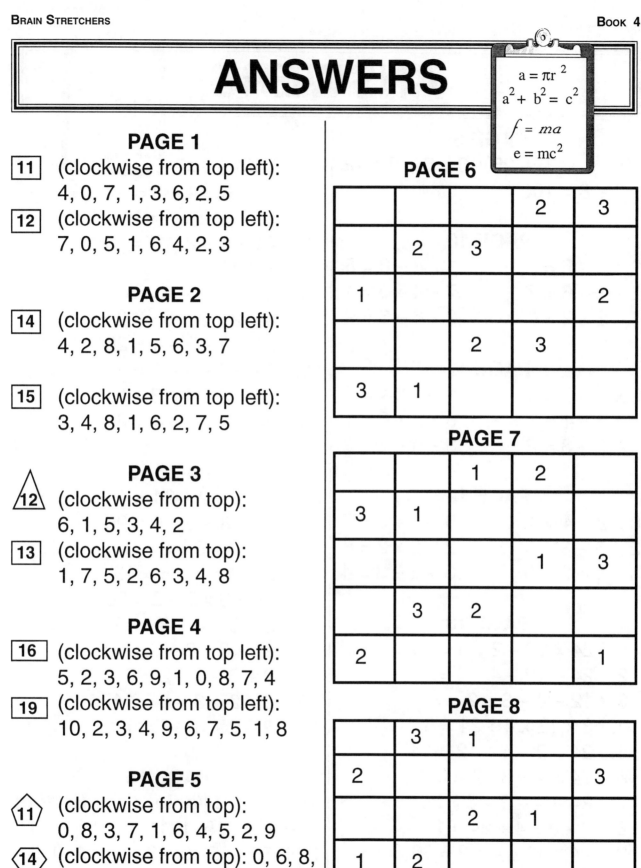

PAGE 6

			2	3
	2	3		
1				2
		2	3	
3	1			

PAGE 7

		1	2	
3	1			
			1	3
	3	2		
2				1

PAGE 8

	3	1		
2				3
		2	1	
1	2			
			3	2

ANSWERS

$$a = \pi r^2$$
$$a^2 + b^2 = c^2$$
$$f = ma$$
$$e = mc^2$$

PAGE 9

$20 + 5 + 10 + 25 + 3 + 6 + 9 + 12$
$+ 2 + 8 = 100$

PAGE 10

$6 + 8 - 5 = 9$ $\qquad$ $1 \times 8 - 3 = 5$
$2 - 1 + 6 = 7$ $\qquad$ $7 - 4 \div 3 = 1$
$4 - 2 - 2 = 0$ $\qquad$ $2 \times 6 - 3 = 9$

PAGE 11

$5 \times 6 \div 6 = 5$ $\qquad$ $9 - 7 \times 4 = 8$
$3 \times 2 - 4 = 2$ $\qquad$ $3 \times 2 \div 6 = 1$
$2 + 3 - 3 = 2$ $\qquad$ $3 + 4 - 5 = 2$

PAGE 12

$8 \times 2 \div 4 = 4$ $\qquad$ $9 + 1 \div 2 = 5$
$2 + 6 - 3 = 5$ $\qquad$ $2 + 2 \times 2 = 8$
$5 + 1 + 3 = 9$ $\qquad$ $3 + 4 - 3 = 4$

PAGE 13

1. $24 \times 12 \div 2 \div 3 = 48$
2. $24 - 12 - 4 - 3 = 5$
3. $12 - 4 - 3 + 2 = 7$
4. $3 \times 12 \times 4 \div 24 = 6$
5. $24 \div 3 \div 4 + 12 = 14$
6. $24 \div 4 \div 3 - 2 = 0$
7. $24 - 4 + 2 + 3 = 25$
8. $2 \times 3 \times 4 \div 24 = 1$
9. $24 \times 12 \div 4 \div 2 = 36$
10. $24 + 2 - 3 - 12 = 11$

PAGE 14

1. $24 \times 6 \div 4 + 3 = 39$
2. $6 \div 3 \times 2 + 4 = 8$
3. $24 - 6 - 2 - 3 = 13$
4. $2 \times 24 \div 6 \div 2 = 4$
5. $2 + 3 + 4 - 6 = 3$
6. $4 \div 2 \times 3 + 6 = 12$
7. $24 \div 3 \times 2 + 4 = 20$
8. $24 - 6 - 4 + 3 = 17$
9. $24 \div 2 \div 4 + 3 = 6$
10. $24 \times 2 \div 6 \div 4 = 2$

PAGE 15

1. $6 \times 8 \times 2 \div 24 = 4$
2. $24 \times 8 \div 2 - 6 = 90$
3. $2 + 3 + 6 - 8 = 3$
4. $8 \div 2 + 3 + 6 = 13$
5. $24 \times 6 \times 2 \div 8 = 36$
6. $2 + 3 + 6 + 8 = 19$
7. $24 \times 8 \div 3 \div 2 = 32$
8. $6 + 8 - 3 - 2 = 9$
9. $6 \div 2 + 3 + 8 = 14$
10. $8 \div 2 + 3 - 6 = 1$

PAGE 16

Top			Middle			Bottom	
7	0	5	15	1	11	6	4
2	4	6	5	9	13	1	3	5
3	8	1	7	17	3	2	0

ANSWERS

$$a = \pi r^2$$
$$a^2 + b^2 = c^2$$
$$f = ma$$
$$e = mc^2$$

PAGE 17

Clockwise: 60, 30, 100, 10, 80, 50, 40, 90, 20, 70

PAGE 18

The mystery number is 37.

PAGE 19

12 x 57 = 684
12 x 65 = 780
39 x 56 = 2184

PAGE 20

Possible Answers
198 x 27 = 5346
157 x 28 = 4396
138 x 42 = 5796
186 x 39 = 7254

PAGES 21–22

Answers will vary.

Example:

Select a mystery number	**5**
Double it	10
Subtract 2	8
Multiply by 4	32
Divide by 8	4
Add 1	**5**

PAGE 23

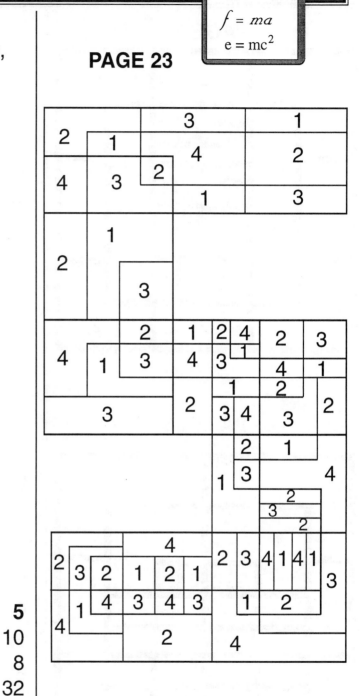

ANSWERS

$$a = \pi r^2$$
$$a^2 + b^2 = c^2$$
$$f = ma$$
$$e = mc^2$$

PAGE 24

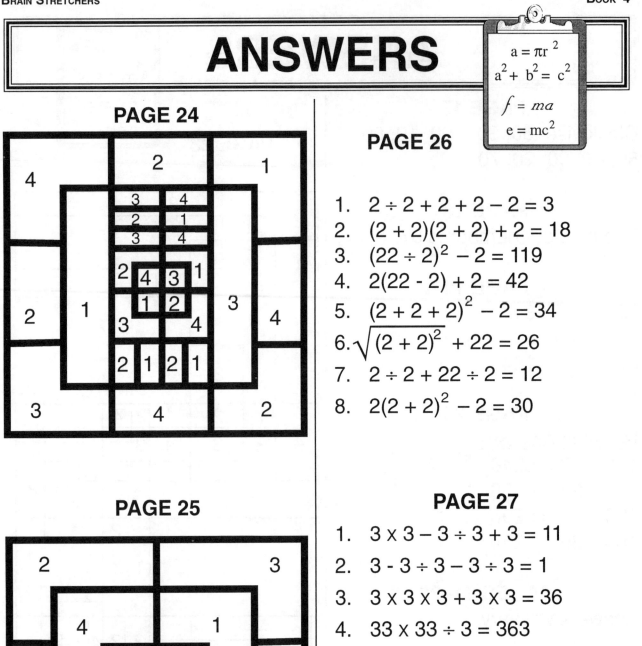

PAGE 26

1. $2 \div 2 + 2 + 2 - 2 = 3$
2. $(2 + 2)(2 + 2) + 2 = 18$
3. $(22 \div 2)^2 - 2 = 119$
4. $2(22 - 2) + 2 = 42$
5. $(2 + 2 + 2)^2 - 2 = 34$
6. $\sqrt{(2 + 2)^2} + 22 = 26$
7. $2 \div 2 + 22 \div 2 = 12$
8. $2(2 + 2)^2 - 2 = 30$

PAGE 25

PAGE 27

1. $3 \times 3 - 3 \div 3 + 3 = 11$
2. $3 - 3 \div 3 - 3 \div 3 = 1$
3. $3 \times 3 \times 3 + 3 \times 3 = 36$
4. $33 \times 33 \div 3 = 363$
5. $33 + 3 \div 3 - 3 = 31$
6. $33^3 \div 3^3 + 33 = 44$
7. $3(3 \div 3 + 3) + 3 = 15$
8. $3 \quad + 3 \quad - 3 = 51$

ANSWERS

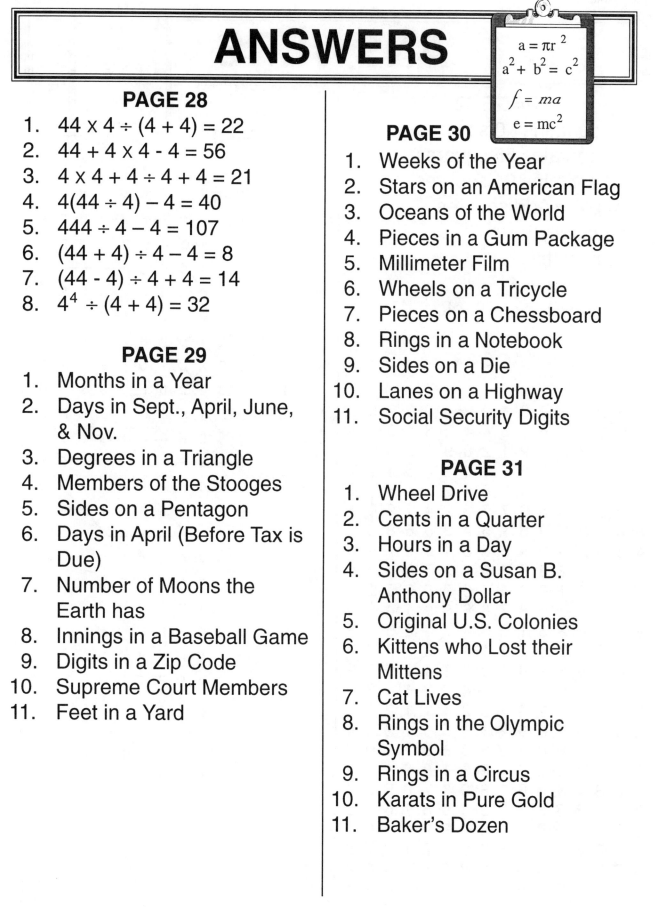

PAGE 28

1. $44 \times 4 \div (4 + 4) = 22$
2. $44 + 4 \times 4 - 4 = 56$
3. $4 \times 4 + 4 \div 4 + 4 = 21$
4. $4(44 \div 4) - 4 = 40$
5. $444 \div 4 - 4 = 107$
6. $(44 + 4) \div 4 - 4 = 8$
7. $(44 - 4) \div 4 + 4 = 14$
8. $4^4 \div (4 + 4) = 32$

PAGE 29

1. Months in a Year
2. Days in Sept., April, June, & Nov.
3. Degrees in a Triangle
4. Members of the Stooges
5. Sides on a Pentagon
6. Days in April (Before Tax is Due)
7. Number of Moons the Earth has
8. Innings in a Baseball Game
9. Digits in a Zip Code
10. Supreme Court Members
11. Feet in a Yard

PAGE 30

1. Weeks of the Year
2. Stars on an American Flag
3. Oceans of the World
4. Pieces in a Gum Package
5. Millimeter Film
6. Wheels on a Tricycle
7. Pieces on a Chessboard
8. Rings in a Notebook
9. Sides on a Die
10. Lanes on a Highway
11. Social Security Digits

PAGE 31

1. Wheel Drive
2. Cents in a Quarter
3. Hours in a Day
4. Sides on a Susan B. Anthony Dollar
5. Original U.S. Colonies
6. Kittens who Lost their Mittens
7. Cat Lives
8. Rings in the Olympic Symbol
9. Rings in a Circus
10. Karats in Pure Gold
11. Baker's Dozen

ANSWERS

$$a = \pi r^2$$
$$a^2 + b^2 = c^2$$
$$f = ma$$
$$e = mc^2$$

PAGE 32

4 x 4 contains 30 squares
5 x 5 contains 55 squares
6 x 6 contains 91 squares
Formula = Add squares
sequentially.
Example: 1
       1 + 4
       1 + 4 + 9, etc.

PAGE 33

PAGE 34

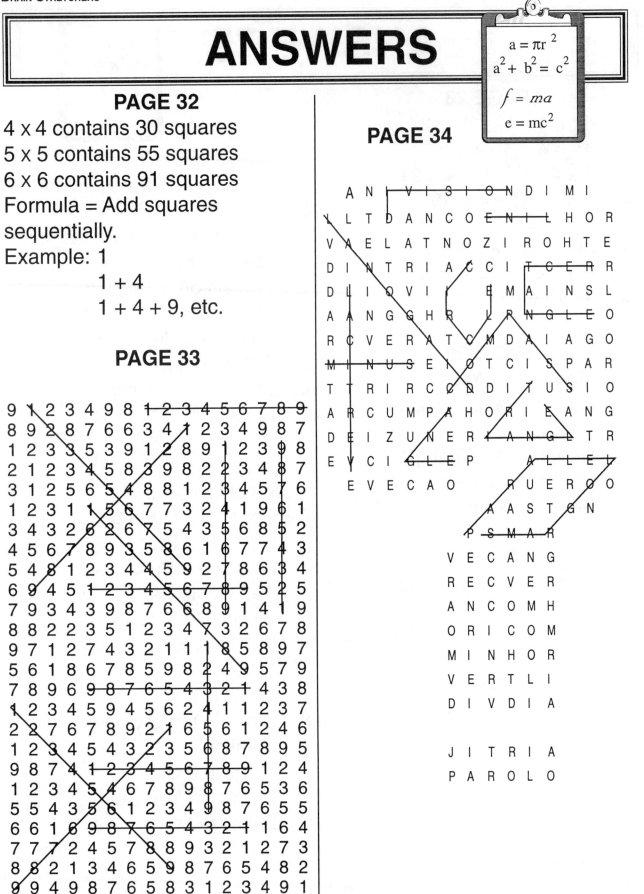

ANSWERS

$$a = \pi r^2$$
$$a^2 + b^2 = c^2$$
$$f = ma$$
$$e = mc^2$$

PAGE 35

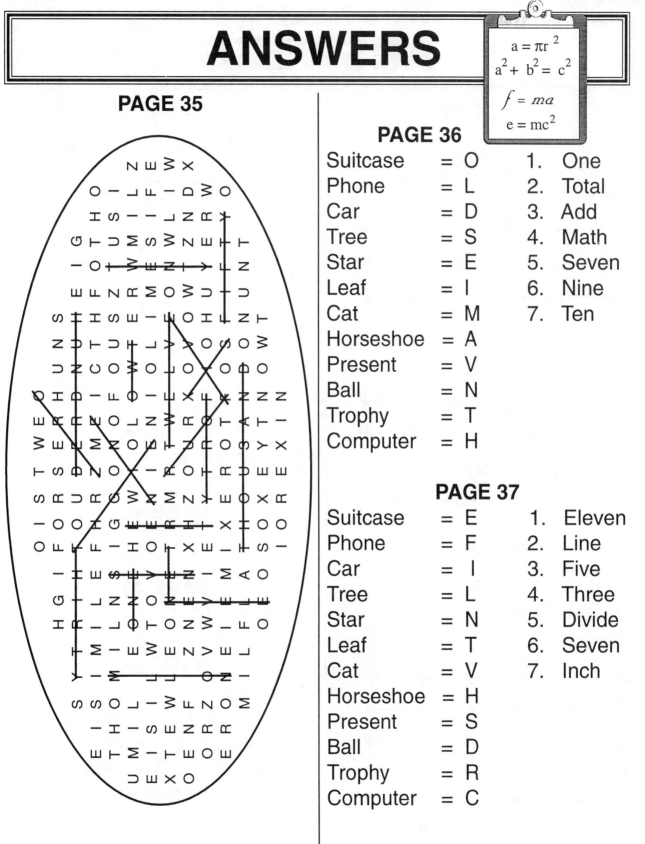

PAGE 36

Suitcase	= O		1.	One
Phone	= L		2.	Total
Car	= D		3.	Add
Tree	= S		4.	Math
Star	= E		5.	Seven
Leaf	= I		6.	Nine
Cat	= M		7.	Ten
Horseshoe	= A			
Present	= V			
Ball	= N			
Trophy	= T			
Computer	= H			

PAGE 37

Suitcase	= E		1.	Eleven
Phone	= F		2.	Line
Car	= I		3.	Five
Tree	= L		4.	Three
Star	= N		5.	Divide
Leaf	= T		6.	Seven
Cat	= V		7.	Inch
Horseshoe	= H			
Present	= S			
Ball	= D			
Trophy	= R			
Computer	= C			

ANSWERS

$$a = \pi r^2$$
$$a^2 + b^2 = c^2$$
$$f = ma$$
$$e = mc^2$$

PAGE 38

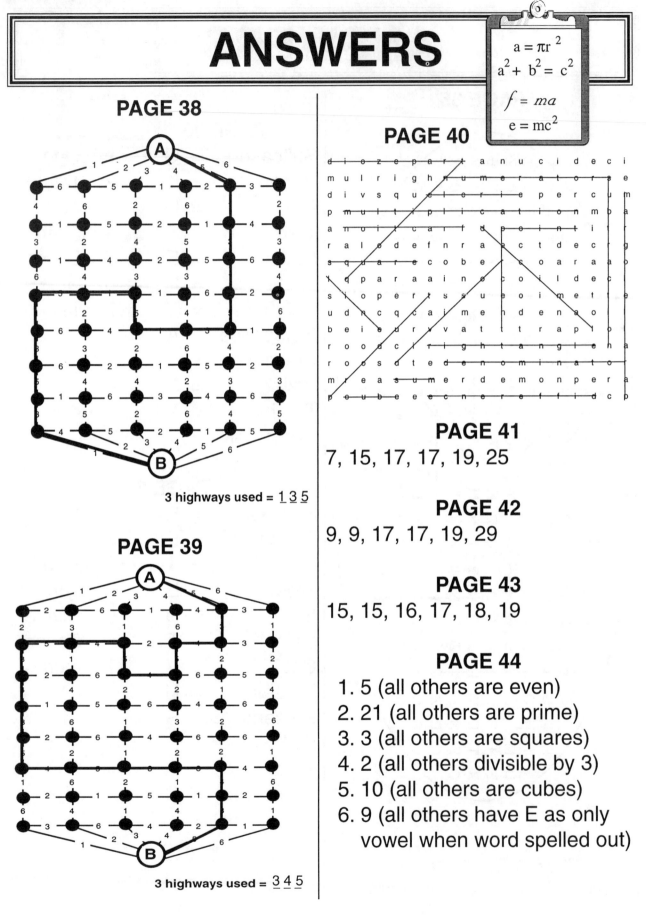

3 highways used = <u>1</u> <u>3</u> <u>5</u>

PAGE 39

3 highways used = <u>3</u> <u>4</u> <u>5</u>

PAGE 40

PAGE 41
7, 15, 17, 17, 19, 25

PAGE 42
9, 9, 17, 17, 19, 29

PAGE 43
15, 15, 16, 17, 18, 19

PAGE 44
1. 5 (all others are even)
2. 21 (all others are prime)
3. 3 (all others are squares)
4. 2 (all others divisible by 3)
5. 10 (all others are cubes)
6. 9 (all others have E as only vowel when word spelled out)

ANSWERS

$$a = \pi r^2$$
$$a^2 + b^2 = c^2$$
$$f = ma$$
$$e = mc^2$$

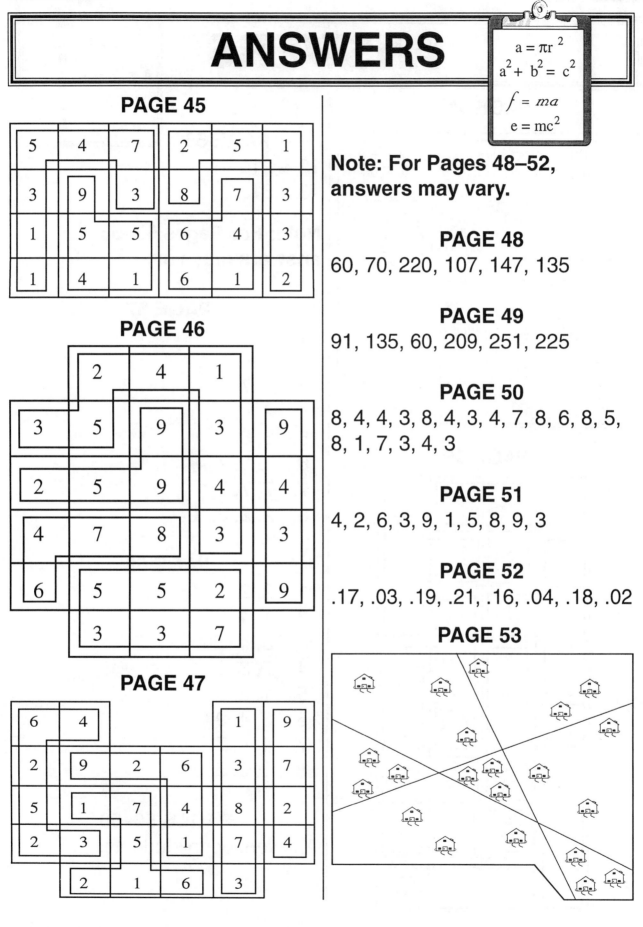

PAGE 45

PAGE 46

PAGE 47

Note: For Pages 48–52, answers may vary.

PAGE 48
60, 70, 220, 107, 147, 135

PAGE 49
91, 135, 60, 209, 251, 225

PAGE 50
8, 4, 4, 3, 8, 4, 3, 4, 7, 8, 6, 8, 5, 8, 1, 7, 3, 4, 3

PAGE 51
4, 2, 6, 3, 9, 1, 5, 8, 9, 3

PAGE 52
.17, .03, .19, .21, .16, .04, .18, .02

PAGE 53

ANSWERS

$a = \pi r^2$
$a^2 + b^2 = c^2$
$f = ma$
$e = mc^2$

PAGE 54

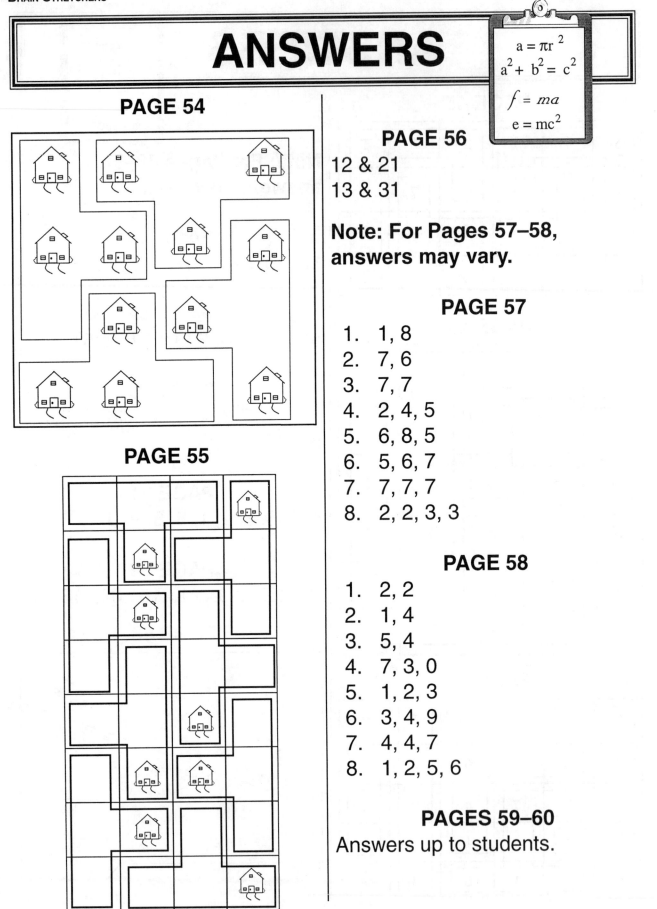

PAGE 55

PAGE 56

12 & 21
13 & 31

Note: For Pages 57–58, answers may vary.

PAGE 57

1. 1, 8
2. 7, 6
3. 7, 7
4. 2, 4, 5
5. 6, 8, 5
6. 5, 6, 7
7. 7, 7, 7
8. 2, 2, 3, 3

PAGE 58

1. 2, 2
2. 1, 4
3. 5, 4
4. 7, 3, 0
5. 1, 2, 3
6. 3, 4, 9
7. 4, 4, 7
8. 1, 2, 5, 6

PAGES 59–60

Answers up to students.